BOOTS

The Story of a Beagle Hound

Boots with his sleepy brother

BOOTS
THE STORY OF A BEAGLE HOUND

Peggy Nicholls

The Book Guild Ltd.
Sussex, England

This book is sold subject to the condition that it shall not, by way of trade or otherwise, be lent, re-sold, hired out, photocopied or held in any retrieval system or otherwise circulated without the publisher's prior consent in any form of binding or cover other than that in which this is published and without a similar condition including this condition being imposed on the subsequent purchaser.

The Book Guild Ltd.
25 High Street,
Lewes, Sussex

First published 1993
© Peggy Nicholls 1993

Set in Baskerville

Typesetting by Raven Typesetters
Ellesmere Port, South Wirral

Printed in Great Britain by
Antony Rowe Ltd.
Chippenham, Wiltshire.

A catalogue record for this book is
available from the British Library

ISBN 0 86332 857 1

CONTENTS

Prologue	There was always a dog in the house	7
Chapter 1	A dog of our own – at last	11
Chapter 2	It's just like having a baby	15
Chapter 3	Growing pains	21
Chapter 4	Training classes	24
Chapter 5	He'll be better when he's two	29
Chapter 6	Some signs of growing up	32
Chapter 7	In his prime	37
Chapter 8	The rescue	41
Chapter 9	Adoption	47
Chapter 10	A new lease of life	53
Chapter 11	Too tired to go on	60
Chapter 12	Free to roam in the forest he loved	66
Chapter 13	Afterwards	69
Chapter 14	And then came Joe	73
Epilogue	He'll always be with us	79

To Peter, my husband, because of Boots

PROLOGUE

There was always a dog in the house

I grew up with dogs. Looking back to my childhood and teenage years, there always seemed to be a dog in the house.

First there was Trixie the wire-haired terrier, but I don't have any particular memories of her – I just knew that she was part of the family. Then a big black Labrador was brought home by my father because she needed to be loved. Peggy was her name, the same as mine, and so it became Peggy the girl and Peggy the dog. The day the vet came for her is etched on my memory. She had become too old and too ill to go on and it was the first time that I saw my father weep. After that came the greyhounds. Father liked to 'go to the dogs' and 'have a flutter'. He really enjoyed going to the dog track and eventually realized his dream to become 'an Owner'. Various, and varied, greyhounds then came home to live out their days with us after their racing careers came to an end.

There was one very special greyhound that we had from the day he was old enough to leave his mother. Father had decided that he wanted a 'new' dog, having previously acquired his racing hounds 'secondhand'. We all went in the car to view the litter and mother chose a light-tan coloured pup which then joined us in the car for the journey back to our home. His pet name was Jimmy and his racing name was Rosie's Choice because mother had decided which puppy 'looked the best'.

Jimmy very quickly became one of the family and was, of course, thoroughly spoilt. When he was old enough he went to live in the racing kennels. We missed him dreadfully, but father hoped that with Jimmy he would have a real champion!

Jimmy loved to rush around the track in hot pursuit of the 'hare' and he easily won his first few races. Unfortunately, and sadly for father, Jimmy had really learned to play and to enjoy life whilst living with us. This led to his subsequent races being disastrous as our lovely hound tried to play with the other dogs as they raced fiercely round the track. He was allowed a few chances, but was eventually banned from the track because he 'turned his head' and put the rest of the field off their purpose – to do their utmost to win the race. And so it was that Jimmy came home much sooner than we had expected. Needless to say we, the children, were delighted with this state of affairs and, once he had got over the initial disappointment, father also seemed happy to have that beautiful greyhound in the bosom of the family once more.

Sadly, Jimmy did not live to a ripe old age. As I have said, we loved having him at home and used to be taken by him for long walks across the surrounding farm land. My brother and I never allowed Jimmy off the lead when we were alone with him. This was because we knew that once our greyhound took flight we would never catch up with him. However, when my father was walking him Jimmy had a wonderful time. He was devoted to his master and would always come when called. Because of this he was able to really explore the countryside to his heart's content. After one such outing, Jimmy became violently and suddenly ill. Before the vet could be summoned our beautiful pet had died.

We were all absolutely shattered. Jimmy was only about five years old and he was very much in his prime. 'What happened?' we demanded to know of my father. He, poor man, was so distraught at the so sudden demise of a lovely, healthy creature, that he could not quickly provide us with the answers we insisted upon. We later learned that Jimmy had, whilst foraging, picked up some strong form of poison.

Ours was a very sad home during the following weeks – indeed months – and we could not quickly take on another dog, although there was a very big gap in the family, as ours was a truly doggie household!

We were, at that time, living next door to my paternal grandparents. They, too, always had a dog in the house, usually an Airedale. My grandmother died and grandfather went to live with his daughter. Flossie, the latest in a long line of Airedales, could not go with him and so, naturally, she came to live with us.

By now I was in my early twenties and courting seriously. Flossie always came to the park or to wherever our walking-out took us. As soon as we sat down and my boyfriend put his arm round me, Flossie climbed onto my lap to establish her prior claims to my affections. She was devoted to my father whose work took him to India for several years. Flossie was growing old and, sadly, she died the day father left India for home. I had recently married but had continued to take Flossie for her daily walks. She was sorely missed, and the kitten brought home by my new husband, though beautiful, could not fill the gap left by my grandparents' last Airedale.

1

A dog of our own – at last

The kitten grew into a cat and for seven years he was loved and cossetted. However, he was never strong and on our seventh wedding anniversary he died, leaving two sad people to mourn his all too early demise.

Six months later Willum arrived. A part-grown tabby, he seemed to have mislaid his home. We tried, but could not find his owners, and so he stayed with us. Another animal to be cared for, but still not a dog, and the discussion as to whether we should, or should not, take on such a responsibility was a weekly occurence.

I wanted one quite desperately, but my husband could look at the matter less emotionally and foresaw many problems. The final decider was, always, Willum, who was now king of all he surveyed. Would Willum mind if we had a dog? As he was originally a stray, and still very much given to disappearing for days on end, we always came to the conclusion that the risk of introducing another animal into the home was too great. It would be terrible if Willum went and did not return.

But then it happened, as we sat watching a film on the television with a doggie performance that tore at the heart strings! 'We must have a dog,' I shouted. My husband was so amazed by my outburst that he instantly agreed, and we decided that Willum as long as he remained King Cat, would be content.

That was on Saturday, but would things have changed by

Monday when it had been decided that we should study our local newspaper. Nothing did change and on Monday evening there we were, gobbling our evening meal, and poring over the advertisements of puppies for sale.

We had seriously intended to have a boxer or a Labrador, having heard and read of their friendly dispositions. However, after Afghan came beagle.

'What about a beagle?' asked my husband.

'What is a beagle?' I replied. Having been told that it was a foxhound with longer ears and shorter legs I still could not form a very clear picture. As, however, I had decided long ago that any dog would suffice, we set off for the home of the beagle breeder.

From two litters there were only two dogs left. One was dozey and cuddly and was coloured apricot and white, the other tricolour, wide awake and rather bombastic. He proceeded to bite his sleepy little brother, pester his long-suffering mother and climb all over us.

'Spend some time with them both,' said the breeder, a very nice lady, 'because you're not choosing a coat that will soon be discarded. This puppy will become a part of your lives and will be with you for many years. It is very important to choose the right one for you.'

We did as she said and studied each puppy in turn, but both of us knew that our minds had really been made up as soon as that little face with the too-big ears had appeared round the hall door to see who was arriving. After my husband had very firmly turned down my suggestion that we should take both puppies, it became obvious that we would leave the docile, sleepy little chap with his mother and take the other one.

We had not expected to actually take the new puppy away with us that evening, and were in no way prepared. Nevertheless, my husband and the lady tucked the eight-week-old beagle into my coat and home we went, taking with us a long diet sheet and leaving an equally long pedigree to be collected the following day. I was certain, on the way home, that the puppy had stopped breathing – a typically maternal reaction – but my spouse studied the furry bundle and assured me that my fears were groundless. And so Boots came home. 'Why Boots?' people were to ask through the coming weeks. We couldn't explain – it just felt right.

I telephoned my mother immediately to report the news of an addition to the family. During our conversation Boots chewed a button from my coat, laddered my tights and then set to work on the hearth rug. Life with our beagle had really begun!

We had been advised by the breeder not to go to the expense of buying a basket for the puppy, and that a cardboard box with a warm piece of material inside would more than suffice. I later realised that she knew the destructive powers of the beagle breed. Having prepared a snug little bed for the puppy, and as it was, by now, getting very late, we settled him into the box and out he popped. We let him explore the room some more, then tried again to put him to bed. It eventually became apparent that if anybody was to sleep that night, Boots must be allowed to select his own bed. After much struggling and with some help from us, he managed to clamber onto the settee and chose a corner of it for himself. We found a car rug both to protect the furniture and make the puppy more comfortable, then we crept off to the bedroom in the early hours of the morning.

Twice during the night the noises from the sitting room compelled us to get up to investigate. On each occasion the puppy had to be cuddled, soothed with warm milk and tucked up in his settee corner once more. But that was just not enough. We had to play with him. Nothing gentle and calming, but a real rough and tumble was demanded of us before Boots would once more allow us to go back to bed. We ought to have realized at that stage that when we wanted to sleep the puppy would want to play. But, blinded by first love, we did not see the writing on the wall!

Could that be the alarm? Surely the night wasn't over – we had hardly slept. Struggling to keep our eyes open we went to admire the new arrival, and were met by very strange smells. We hastily gathered up the strategically placed newspapers, upon which Boots had, or rather he should have, made his puddles and piles. We soon discovered where he had tried and missed! How hard, we wondered, had our puppy tried when he appeared to have missed so often? Because he was only a baby we had to make allowances, but the carpet became increasingly soggy and somewhat smelly. We decided to watch him closely. Boots would be deeply engrossed in the delight of the moment, would feel the urge to 'go' and would rush towards the nearest newspaper. As soon as his front paws had landed on the paper, he would 'perform'. He never did seem to work out that two front paws on the paper were just not enough!

We decided that Boots had to be introduced to our neighbours without further delay. We were still quite young in those days, and on each side of us were couples coming up to retirement age. This meant that we were very much regarded as the 'youngsters' in the row and, as such, received a lot of kindly advice and assistance!

Before settling the puppy down that day, I sat him in the crook of my arm and sallied forth. First to the neighbours to the left of us who were, indeed, interested in the addition to our family. What they could not accept, however, was his name. 'Fancy calling a pedigree dog Boots,' they said. 'Doesn't he have a kennel name?' they asked. 'Yes, Anjuline Jason,' we replied. 'That's it – call him Jason,' they decided, adding that they felt 'Jason' to be more fitting to our little dog's breeding. Fortunately they were not offended when they later learned that we had stuck determinedly to 'Boots' feeling it to be a name of distinction and character!

The neighbours to the right of us just went overboard when they met the new little creature from next door. Offers to mind him came thick and fast and, for as long as we stayed in that bungalow, Boots was loved and admired by all around.

2

It's just like having a baby

'But it's just like having a baby in the house.' How often we were to hear those words during the ensuing weeks. We had never had a baby, but could now begin to understand the hollow-eyed, sometimes desperate looks on the faces of friends new to parenthood.

We studied the diet sheet that had been handed to us with the puppy, with strict instructions from the breeder not to deviate from the directions thereon! We then made out a shopping list and began to realize something of the cost of having a dog in the house. As most of the items came in the babyfood range, we felt the expense incurred by a puppy must be comparable to that of having a baby! The comparisons seemed, repeatedly, to be between puppy and baby.

With a very long shopping list in his hand my husband went off to work via the local chemist's shop. He was to receive many sympathetic glances from the assistant on his increasingly more tired visits for rusks and baby cereal. He never did explain that the wear and tear were due to a puppy and not to a baby!

Feeds had to be measured and mixed five times a day, at regular intervals. The meat and milk feeds must be given at different times, and fresh eggs had to be included several times each week. Then there was the special puppy mixture containing calcium that had to be added to each meal to ensure that the puppy grew strong, healthy bones. Last, but by no means least, he had to have six vitamin pills each day, which must never be forgotten.

What amazed us, with hindsight, was that whilst we were sticking so rigidly to this exacting diet for our beagle, he was eating everything he could get his teeth to! Strange as it may seem it never occurred to us that, as he was eating carpets, chairs, slippers – you name it and he was eating it – it might not be absolutely necessary to continue feeding him on a diet designed for a tender young digestion. We had never, you understand, been responsible for a puppy before, and we intended to stick to the rules and not to fail in any respect, come what may! However, as the weeks went by we did become somewhat lax regarding Boots' vitamins. We knew that dogs require vitamins A and D and B complex. The tablets contained a large amount of the latter, being yeast-based, and Boots ate them like sweets. However, as he was eating so voraciously and seemed to be so well – positively bursting with good health – we did become negligent regarding the required six pills a day. Some days he had the prescribed amount, but more often, he only had two or three. We did notice that he was tending to become over-excited and decidedly wound-up about certain things. This was especially noticeable if he had stolen something and we were trying to retrieve the said article before total destruction set in. If it was food that had been stolen we really did not stand a chance of getting anything back from our beagle. If, on the other hand, it was an article of clothing we could, sometimes, save the garment or enough of it to be repaired and used again. If Boots had stolen a piece of equipment, such as a brush or some household linen, such as a towel, we did not always take up the challenge of trying to discipline our dog. On those occasions much would depend upon our state of fitness for the fray!

In those days my mother-in-law, who had been recently widowed, used to spend a lot of time at our bungalow. She always came to a meal on Sunday and was always in her church-going Sunday best. She was a lovely lady who had quickly grown to love our Boots. She was, however, somewhat bewildered at times by his wayward behaviour – but then so were we!

I shall never forget the Sunday when mother-in-law came home with us after the morning service dressed in her new winter hat and coat. She really did look super and the hat was particularly admired, being made from expensive felt that looked like velvet. Boots took a great fancy to this beautiful creation and removed it from the bedroom. How we could have been careless enough to leave the door open I do not know. He rushed into the sitting room waving the hat around in great glee. Try as we would not one of us could persuade him to let go. The more we entreated, the more we cajoled, the more determined Boots became to hold onto his treasure. What amazed us most was that even the offer of food was not taken up if that meant parting with the hat, and eventually we realized that Boots was actually getting into quite a state – very wound-up indeed. When at last my husband managed to prise the hat away by sheer brute force we were all, Boots and the hat included, in a very sorry state.

The outcome of this episode was that mother-in-law, for the rest of that winter, wore a hat that was so scarred by beagle claws and teeth it looked as though it had been attacked by a tiger at the very least! No matter, she would not let us buy her another one and each Sunday when we sat behind her in church we were reminded of our bad beagle.

Another result of that particular episode was that we questioned why Boots was becoming so worked-up on such occasions. We contacted the lady who bred him only to be closely interrogated about the number of vitamin pills he was having each day. We never again allowed ourselves to lapse in that respect!

I was working part-time at a local hospital when Boots came into the family. This meant being away from home from about 10 a.m. until 5 p.m. on three days each week. We had decided that the puppy could not possibly be left alone for more than three or four hours at a time. This meant that on the days I was away, my husband had to come home at lunch time to feed, clean, exercise and generally spoil the new arrival. He also had to clean and repair the sitting room! We had been told by the breeder that beagles fell into two categories when left alone.

Either Boots would bewail his lot – loudly – or he would seek consolation in destroying things. I hoped desperately that we had not acquired a cry-beagle, both for the sake of our neighbours and also because this would have distressed us. What I did not realize, in my ignorance, was just how much destruction would be necessary in order to provide consolation for our beagle every time he was left!

I am surprised by how small our puppy was when he first came to us. Because of the amazing, indeed the appalling, things he did from the very moment he set paw inside his new home, I began to view him as larger than life-size. This was not so. When I now look at the many photographs taken during those first weeks, I am reminded that he was a very little creature! When I tucked him under my arm he looked just like a cuddly toy.

Wherever we went Boots was admired and positively drooled over. He accepted all of this adulation with gracious indifference. Life was there to be investigated and thoroughly enjoyed and that meant he did not have too much time to waste on people with their funny ways. Right from the beginning our beagle would accept or reject affection, depending upon the excitement of the moment. I don't want to give the impression that he was unloving because beagles have a reputation for being responsive to affection. It was simply that so often there were many inviting distractions and he really did have to get his beagle priorities right. Needless to say we showered him with our love and devotion from the very first and I like to think that this made Boots into an extremely secure and well-adjusted dog.

Until he had had all of his injections, he was not allowed to pound the public pavements. He was, therefore, carried whenever we took him out of the home or garden. The feel of his little warm body was lovely, but very short-lived. As soon as he was able to set paw to communal ground Boots absolutely refused to be carried anywhere. No matter how foul the weather, he trotted along, often ending the journey very wet and covered in mud, but totally content. He looked so small as he strained on his lead and caused many anxious stares from passers by when he repeatedly choked because he was pulling too hard. This worried me partly because I did not like any suggestion that we might not be caring for our puppy correctly, and partly because I was afraid that Boots would damage his throat. Not so, insisted my husband, because if our beagle felt any discomfort he would, surely, stop the constant pulling. We learned, of course, as we went on through life with our dog, that a beagle will put up with any amount of discomfort in order to achieve his ends – whatever they might be! Nevertheless, because of my concern, we bought a harness for Boots. This did not stop him pulling but it did stop the disconcerting choking noises that had previously emanated from him.

From the earliest days Boots made up his mind about what he wanted and then really went all out to achieve his desires! In between his more obviously planned adventures, he would have many rush and grab sessions. Some of these resulted in considerable expense to ourselves as curtains were torn, furniture was shredded and carpets severely molested! A few such occasions will never be forgotten, mainly because of the relief felt by my husband and I when we subsequently had time to have a mental replay of what had happened.

When Boots was three months old my sister had her twenty-first birthday. We wanted to give her something special and lasting and decided to visit the antique shops in Brighton. We hoped to find an opal ring, knowing how much she liked this particular stone and knowing also her penchant for rings. We had been into several shops without success and Boots was really enjoying this new experience when the owner of yet another jewellers invited us to be seated whilst he went through his stock. I very firmly sat our excited puppy on my lap, not realizing that such an action put his little face with its big mouth on a level with the glass-topped counter.

'Here is a particularly pretty stone,' said the kindly sales-man, as he held out an opal ring for our inspection. Before we could catch more than a fleeting glimpse of the said ring Boots made one of his famous lunges in an effort to grab the opal from the man's hand! I screamed – my usual reaction at such times – my husband sprang forward and the jeweller stood transfixed with a look of horror on his face. Somehow the ring was grabbed by a human hand before it quite reached that doggie jaw, but it was a very near thing.

We did purchase a ring from that particular shop, but Boots was taken right away from the counter and from the merchandise, much to his disgust and to the great relief of the owner.

When we thought about the incident afterwards, we realized that we could easily have been paying a great deal of money for an article somewhere inside our dog. We should then, of course, have had to concentrate even more avidly upon his waste disposal! Whether my sister would have enjoyed wearing a ring that had travelled through Boots stomach and bowels, to name only part of its journey, we never discovered, but the incident did make us exceedingly careful whenever our puppy went shopping in the future.

3

Growing pains

In those early months Boots seemed to do everything possible to sabotage my departure for work. New distractions had to be constantly created to enable me to get ready to leave, making sure that I was properly dressed.

The only room where I could achieve a modicum of privacy from our beagle was the bathroom. Each working day I would strive to have enough time shut away to throw on my smart clothes – my non-beagled ones – and drag on my unladdered tights. Each day Boots would keep hurling his little fat body at the bolted door as he frantically tried to get in to have yet another rough and tumble.

One morning I tossed a thick woolly jacket in his direction hoping to distract him for a few minutes. A totally thoughtless, indeed an irresponsible gesture on my part! Within seconds all ten buttons had been ripped from the garment only to disappear with breathtaking speed down Boots' throat. I was appalled! Not, you understand, by the now tattered state of a previously wholesome piece of clothing, but by the sobering thought of the damage that could be done to Boots' insides.

A doctor who saw the anguish on my face as I arrived at the hospital drew me into his office and asked what was wrong. 'It's Boots,' I replied. By some amazing oversight he had not heard of our new arrival, and so looked at my leather-clad legs inquiringly. 'No, no, it's the puppy,' I explained. He then, with great patience, managed to elicit from me the information that the offending buttons were round and smooth and not sharp-edged. I was then sent on my way with the assurances of a Consultant Physician ringing in my ears that all would be well. He was, of course, quite right, although the buttons were never actually seen emerging from our puppy!

During those first few months we heard numerous beagle tales, each more horrifying than its predecessor. There were beagles that strayed, including one that could not even be contained by an electrified fence! Then there were beagles that were destructive – but we had quickly learned all about those. Many beagles seemed to be abandoned, and, most worrying of all, we heard of one that had to be put to sleep because he was uncontrollable.

Although I had grown up with a dog, or dogs, in the family, I had never lived with a hound. There were those who had said that there was no experience that could compare with that particular one. We met people who had had a beagle or, sometimes, beagles, and their reactions to this were always very definite. Some said 'Never again,' or 'We just could not cope,' and others stated firmly and enthusiastically that there was nothing, but nothing, to compare with the personality of a beagle hound.

I have called this chapter 'Growing Pains', and did at first think of this as describing Boots and what he felt during the first months of his life with us. Now, however, I think of it as our 'growing pains' as we learned to live with our beagle. He was beautiful, affectionate, abounding with energy, into absolutely everything, always looking for the next adventure, disobedient, wilful, stubborn and, it had begun to seem, quite untrainable.

We had to get through those first months somehow, having made up our minds that as soon as he was old enough our dog would be taken to be trained by someone more experienced and less pliable than my husband and myself. Perhaps we loved him too much, although I don't really believe so. How could it be possible to give too much love to such a totally loveable creature? I do know that we spoilt him, partly because he seemed to have been born to be spoilt and partly because it was, all too often, our only means of self-preservation. By relaxing our so-called discipline and giving our puppy his own way, we sometimes managed to get some rest and peace for ourselves.

I make it sound as though there was very little enjoyment during those first months, but that would be the wrong impression to give. Boots opened up a whole new world to us and it certainly was not his fault that he had come into our lives at a time when we were very busy with home, work and church activities.

In our determination not to let the new arrival lack in any way, we really did wear ourselves out. By the time Boots was six months old, we were beginning to feel the strain of trying to find enough time to devote to our increasingly demanding puppy. We knew that we had to take stock of our lives and make some serious adjustments. Not once did it occur to us that we should part with our beagle, even though we seemed to be going around in ever decreasing circles. We had taken him on for life and for life we would keep him!

This was not really as dramatically self-sacrificing as it sounds, because within hours of that little bundle of energy bouncing into our home, we had become his slaves. It was not a fair contest, really, because we could tell from the very beginning that he was the master of all he surveyed. Needless to say, that included my husband and myself!

4

Training classes

When Boots was six months old he was taken to training classes. The youngest there, he was also the least co-operative. Even the trainer could not make him 'stay' if he wanted to 'go'. He came bottom of the obedience class, but was easily top in the beauty stakes!

Our beagle did so enjoy his training class evening. It was my husband who actually worked with Boots, and it quickly became apparent that, as I was not actively involved, I could not be present at these sessions. Seeing his 'mum' watching from the sidelines was just too easy an excuse for Boots to become even more extrovert than usual.

He always knew when training evening had arrived, and was put into the car in an already excited state. As the other owners walked sedately through the swing doors, their dogs walking to heel, Boots and my husband arrived with the stretched length of the lead between them. No amount of bellowing or cajoling could ever stop our beagle from erupting panting into the Village Hall with his master still on the wrong side of the doors. After each session both master and dog arrived home exhausted and mute – the one from shouting orders that were usually ignored and the other from the sheer enjoyment of it all!

One evening, before we had decided that my presence was definitely counter-productive, I was sitting watching from the sidelines. All ten dogs were lined up with their owners beside them. The trainer instructed the latter to order their respective pets to 'stay' and then to walk away, each one hoping that his dog would perform well and remain in its place.

My husband gave Boots the necessary command, and with a show of confidence, walked away. Within moments our dog had leapt to his feet. I expected him to rush after his master but he had other plans, and began very solemnly to study the dog next door, an Airedale that was 'staying' most impressively. We had, after only a few weeks, decided that this particular dog was in the running for top place at the end of the training course. I have to confess that the Airedale's hopes of fame, or rather those of his master, were to be dashed. Boots walked up to him and waited for a reaction. When there was nothing forthcoming, our naughty little dog lifted his large paw and soundly smacked the other dog on the nose! That was just too much for the poor Airedale who leapt to his feet ready for the rough and tumble to commence. Chaos quickly followed when the rest of the doggie line-up joined in. Needless to say, Boots was not number one favourite that evening with the trainer!

On another evening the order was for the dogs to 'lie and stay' whilst their owners walked into the centre of the hall. That was just too much for Boots to accept, and he repeatedly

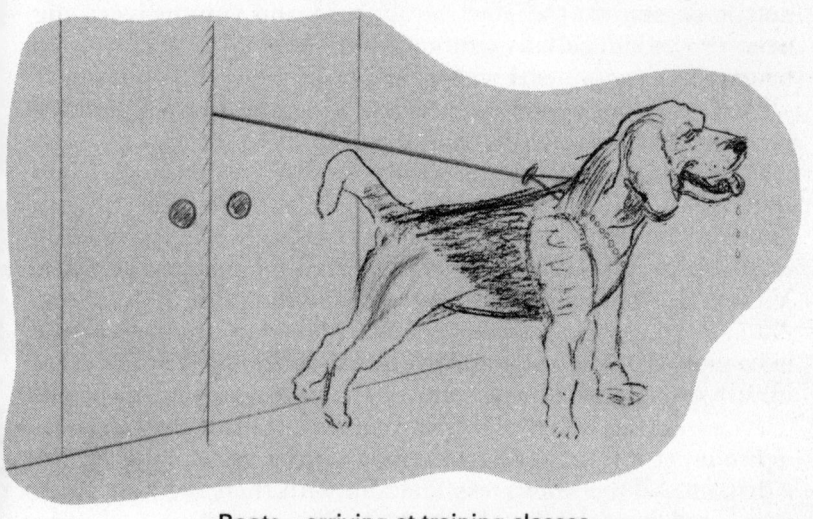

Boots – arriving at training classes

trotted after my husband who became increasingly embarrassed by the situation. 'Give him to me,' said the trainer, who made a point of using the wayward dogs as training fodder. She was a very determined lady who believed that dogs should be trained on the choke collar or chain. We were not happy with this particular piece of equipment and it was firmly discarded once the training classes had ended, but, on the night in question, Boots was duly wearing his training 'uniform'. My husband obediently handed over our dog to the trainer, who had obviously made up her mind to bring this disobedient beagle to heel. Boots had other ideas! No matter how much she commanded, no matter how much she choked him, he simply refused to obey. Every ounce of his beagle stubbornness came into play! The more red of face the trainer became the more Boots threw himself onto his back, legs waving enthusiastically in the air. Eventually he was almost thrown back to my husband with the comment, 'He's too playful.'

At the end of the course the prizes were handed out. A bull terrier came first – the Airedale was second and Boots, our beautiful beagle, was right down there at the bottom of the class. When the trainer suggested to my husband that he and our little one should start afresh with the new trainees, the answer was a decidedly emphatic 'No'. Boots was not given the choice. He had learned what to do, and when to do it – or not to do it – but, as we soon discovered, he would only put this acquired knowledge into practise if he felt so inclined. There were good beagle days and there were bad beagle days. There were also very bad beagle days! On one such day I found him standing on a chair in the kitchen, front paws just reaching the unit, eating his way through the birthday cake I had made for a colleague. He wasn't sick – he rarely was at such times – but I had to set to and make another cake, blaming myself for leaving a chair too close to the cupboard. With hindsight I realise that I didn't often chastise our puppy because it was usually all too easy to find an excuse for his badness. A few days after the episode of the cake, my husband decided to put up the Christmas decorations. As fast as a streamer or paper chain appeared from the box, Boots grabbed it and destroyed it. He was particularly interested in the fairy lights. It soon became obvious that Boots had to be removed from the scene if any decorating was to be achieved. It also became apparent that everything must be placed above dog height or reach.

When Boots and I returned from our very long walk round the block – it was an extremely cold night – I thought my husband had decided not to deal with the decorations after all. Not so – once I had been instructed to raise my eyes above seven feet from the ground, I saw that everything, including the lights, was arranged around the top of the room. The ceiling looked very pretty and reminded me of the sky at night. Even Boots couldn't take the lights down from that height!

Through all of these adventures and misadventures Boots grew – indeed he flourished. We wilted, but struggled on, as our sitting room changed from a place of peaceful charm into a bare room with two chairs, a television set and underlay on the floor; the coming of Boots completely changed not only our home but our whole way of life.

Certain things, such as work, had of course to continue. It did, however, become increasingly difficult to get to hospital and office on time, which meant staying on later to get the work done. Our church commitments also had to be honoured, but our social life totally disintegrated. When we had time to ourselves it was given over completely to the puppy. Boots demanded our full attention, which meant that such pleasures as watching the television or enjoying a relaxed meal together became the exception rather than the rule!

Food could no longer be eaten from trays whilst seated in a comfortable chair because, small though he was, Boots managed to clear one's plate before knife and fork could be brought into play. Meals had to be eaten at table, having first made sure that both table and chairs were far enough away from any other piece of furniture to make it impossible for our beagle to leap upon us or the food.

Just as he found meal times a challenge so also did he look upon sitting down to watch the television as a signal to become as boisterous and destructive as possible! The one programme we persisted in trying to watch was *Colditz*. My husband and I would seat ourselves in the two remaining chairs having first plugged in the TV set. Wherever he was in the bungalow our beagle would hear that stirring signature tune and would then proceed to hurl himself into the room and rush straight across it to the corner housing the television. He would then grab the cable knowing full well that we would both, simultaneously, hurtle towards the same spot in a united and frenzied effort to prevent our wicked little dog from electrocuting himself. We would then encourage him to sit with us whilst we watched the programme, but always to no avail. As soon as the restraining hand relaxed Boots would leap down, bolt across to the television and try to chew the cable. We eventually worked out that the only way to control our dog was to put him on his lead and sit him on one of our laps. However, whichever one of us drew the short straw had then to put on very thick gloves because Boots proceeded to bite furiously at the hands that were holding him and his baby teeth were lethal!

All of which makes it sound that, small though he was, we really could not control our beagle puppy with any real success. That was, indeed, the truth of it. Perhaps we should have been firmer – we did try – but suffice it to say that Boots invariably emerged from these encounters and experiences looking every inch the victor. We, on the other hand, were usually exhausted, bitten, frustrated and defeated. Despite this we were still totally besotted with our beautiful, bouncy beagle.

5

He'll be better when he's two

The first two years of Boots' life were frenetic – for us, that is, not for him. He obviously loved each and every joyous waking moment. He had a great urge to destroy things, which meant that when he was not sleeping or eating, he had to be tearing something apart!

We assumed that he was getting enough sleep, although when we were around it was always 'all systems go'. He demanded our attention constantly. Also, the havoc that he wrought each time he was left alone strongly suggested that he had been very busy during the few hours we were away.

On the days when my husband came home at lunchtime Boots was taken to a local park where he exercised with six other beagles. (The breed was very fashionable at that time.) This meant that our beagle puppy had a riotous time being pushed about by this beagle 'pack', whilst being thoroughly spoilt by the other doting owners. He would then be taken home, cleaned up or washed down, depending upon the state of the day, then tucked up for the few hours remaining before my own return from work. Whether the lunchtimes were just too exciting for him or whether he was just born to be bad, we were not sure. Suffice it to say that on each of my long days away from home, I found chaos and destruction on my return.

As I stepped into the sitting room an energetic ball of beagle would hurl itself at me. The usual love-in followed, much enjoyed by us both. Then would come my feeling of appalled disbelief as I looked around. How could such a little animal achieve so much in such a short time? The energy he must have expended to bring about such a shambles was awesome to contemplate.

On one occasion I wondered why, in the fading light, the sitting room carpet looked dark grey instead of its normal bright cream colour. As the lights went on I felt stunned. The six foot studio couch had been dragged into the middle of the room and the top mattress pulled off. This had then been slit from end to end and its horsehair stuffing had been removed and spread all over the floor. Whilst I stood rooted to the spot and quite speechless, Boots ran around gathering up pieces of said stuffing. When he turned that beautiful beagle face towards me he looked like a doggie dwarf from Snow White with the horsehair making a bristly beard around his little jowl. Not knowing where to begin I telephoned my husband. These increasingly frequent calls at the climax of his busy working day were beginning to put a lot of pressure upon him. So much so that my mother suggested the anguished telephone calls should be made to her instead. One thing was certain, and that was that somebody had to receive a call from me so that I could give vent to my feelings of appalled amazement at the havoc being wrought in our home!

I could never really say that I was angry, because Boots was altogether too beautiful and loveable to arouse such a feeling. What I just could not believe, but what my eyes repeatedly told me I had to believe, was that our puppy was an undiscerning destroyer of anything and everything that came within his grasp. One thing I did have to accept, and very quickly, was that all electrical goods had to be disconnected when Boots was to be left alone. I learned this lesson one day when I arrived home, bent down to plug in a lamp, was practically knocked over by the bang and the flash and discovered that I had a blackened hand and that I was shaking from head to toe. The flex had been almost severed by beagle teeth and I was very fortunate to be still in one piece!

The chewing and the destruction continued long after puppy teeth had been replaced by adult molars. Those who knew about such things assured us that our wayward beagle would be better when he reached his second birthday and we looked with increasingly hopeful hearts towards the 16th of July, 1974.

To be on the safe side we had bought him an indestructible ball for that special anniversary. The day dawned, the ball was received with great enthusiasm and we held our respective breaths. Within minutes the supposedly unchewable object had been masticated into an unrecognisable mass! It was then that we realized with deepening disappointment that our beautiful, destroying beagle would not have a sudden personality change now that he was two. The process was, in fact, very much more gradual, and he never completely stopped stealing and eating such things as shoes and tights. Providing, however, that we kept alert and one step ahead in awareness, we discovered that less foreign bodies passed through his system as the years went by.

6

Some signs of growing up

Between the age of two and five years Boots seemed to show some signs of growing up – not many – but every show of obedience was wildly rewarded! His energy was boundless and each waking moment had to be filled. Life was one great big adventure to him and, because we were totally besotted, to us also. The difference was that he rarely tired whereas we seemed to be constantly exhausted. He was absolutely secure and completely uninhibited, being afraid of nothing except the noise of the dust cart.

During those years we spent many holidays in the New Forest. Boots soon recognised the signs of packed suitcases and his bed being moved from house to car. He would stand on the back seat, leaning over my husband's shoulder, willing the car along. He always knew when the trees we had been passing through became the beginnings of the Forest. Gradually he grew familiar with an increasing number of special walks. Once visited, a place was always remembered and greeted like an old friend.

One thing we soon learned was that, now we had a beagle, the days were gone when we could stand and stare. All the time that Boots was running free, we had to be either watching him or, more usually, trying to keep up with him. A sudden interesting scent could mean that he would vanish from our sight before we could draw enough breath to tell him to 'stay'. Not that he would have obeyed, if the scent was a good one,

He was afraid of nothing...

because he always got his beagle priorities right!

On one such occasion we had arrived in a part of the Forest that was new to us all. Before we had decided which path to explore, Boots was off. Nose down, tail erect, he had disappeared from our sight within seconds. We were appalled, having no idea where he could be heading because the terrain was new to us. We then realized, with increasing alarm, that the time of year was the rutting season for deer. The noun 'rut' is derived from the words 'to roar', and we were certain that Boots had both picked up a strong scent and also heard the strange noise that had reached our less attuned ears. As we visualised our beagle giving chase, it was impossible to heed the advice we had heard to 'always stay where your beagle left you,' but as there were two of us we took it in turns to patrol the immediate area or plough deeply into the woods. Just to stand around was impossible, but as the minutes and then the hours ticked by, we became more and more anxious. Anxiety then turned into real fright. Never before had he been missing for hours.

Whilst one of us remained on the spot where Boots had left us, the other one searched frantically in ever widening circles.

It was my turn to 'stay' and my husband once more set off into the trees. He was still in sight when I saw him stop, then turn and point excitedly. There coming towards us was Boots, literally down on his beagle knees and utterly exhausted. We could only assume that he had picked up the scent of deer and run for miles through the Forest.

Our relief knew no bounds! We watered him and packed him into the car, then went to have tea. No more adventures for that day, although one thing that the experience had confirmed was that Boots would always return to the same spot where he had last been with us – a thought in which we took great comfort.

During those years a walk was never complete for Boots unless he found a treasure. This could be anything from a plastic bottle to a six foot sapling. The former he would carry, bulging from each side of his jowl, collecting admiring glances from all who passed by. The latter had to be manipulated through the woods and back to the car. He would not leave his prize behind, nor could he always cope with it alone. On many such occasions we had to help our determined little dog to get his latest treasure back home.

He especially liked anything made from rubber – both the smell and the texture obviously appealed to him. Whilst walking by a river one sunny day, Boots came upon a discarded piece of that substance. He was very thrilled and ran hither and thither with it stuffed in his mouth. We had to pass a herd of cows and, before we could even think about remonstrating with him, our beagle had yielded to temptation, plunged into their midst and was doing his imitation of a sheep dog. The cows were not at all pleased by this attempt to round them up! More – they showed definite signs of becoming very cross about it. My husband then became cross because Boots had, not surprisingly, grown suddenly deaf. No amount of bellowing on

Boots – with one of the cows

my husband's part would stop him as cows and husband directed the full force of their combined crossness upon him! At first this simply added to Boots' fun, but he gradually became aware that my husband was very angry indeed and that the cows were certainly not happy. With a great show of offhanded reluctance our beagle detached himself from the cows and rejoined us on the path. Cows quickly forgotten, he looked for his piece of rubber. Where could it be? He searched and searched then looked at us with those big doggie eyes and asked whether we could offer any suggestions. I realized with dismay that he had dropped his treasure amongst the cows. 'Leave it there,' said my husband. 'Please get it for me,' pleaded those beagle eyes. And so, as on many other occasions, I became like putty in his paws, and dived in amongst the still restless beasts to retrieve the rubber. Boots received this with much glee and ran off along the path in front of us.

This incident showed us that if our dog was ever in serious trouble, or was confronted by a problem to which he did not know the answer, he would always expect my husband or I to do something. Needless to say we always tried to oblige and his confidence in us was boundless.

Although our beagle continued to take great delight in

destroying things, by the time he was five years old he had grown into a handsome and even, on occasion, an obedient animal.

7

In his prime

Between his fifth and tenth birthdays Boots was truly in his prime. He was well known in the seaside town where we lived, partly for his good looks, but more especially because of his outgoing and venturesome personality.

His one great failing was that he preferred the balls being thrown for other dogs to those we had given up throwing for him. He would scoop a ball from under the nose of its doggie owner and then flatly refuse to give it back. His hound's hunting instinct would come into play and he would dare anyone to try to retrieve the stolen ball. This would be firmly clamped between his clenched teeth and many was the time when we nearly lost some fingers trying to prise those beagle jaws apart! Other owners usually accepted this unsocial behaviour with good humour, gave their address and received the ball back when Boots' embarrassed owners had managed to bribe him into parting with it. Occasionally, however, an owner would be exceedingly displeased, not to say unpleasant. No matter, Boots would trot around us, letting us all know he had the ball but refusing to return it. Sometimes, as I have said, we managed to find something he liked more than another dog's treasure, and he would then relinquish the ball without losing face. More often however, he would not part with his loot until he was back home. We would then studiously ignore him – Boots never could tolerate this – and he would simply drop the ball, obviously finding no pleasure in keeping it jammed in his mouth if mum and dad had apparently lost interest in trying to retrieve it.

Gradually we learned that the more we tried to persuade him to see things our way, the more determined he would become to do what *he* wanted. This determination, together with his stubbornness, meant that life with our beagle was often very hard work but it was never dull!

During those years our regular visits to the New Forest continued. Occasionally we went elsewhere and there is still a bedroom door in a hotel in Weymouth bearing testimony to the fact that Boots objected, on one occasion, to being left in the room during our meal time. He usually behaved very well when we stayed in a hotel, but we always had to get him across the hallway and out through the front door before he could mark his new-found territory – in laymen's terms that means before he could cock his leg and leave a puddle behind him! Because of his beagle good looks, Boots was always made very welcome and, when he did break the house rules, excuses were quickly forthcoming from our hosts.

Holidays with our beagle were not really relaxing. They were interesting and, seen through his eyes, exciting, but we always had to be on the move. Boots never really learned the art of sitting and letting the world go by. He always wanted to be up front making things happen.

Fortunately we enjoy walking because during the years we lived with Boots that was just what we did. He would accept that picnics had to be eaten whilst stationary, but as soon as the food had gone he would lose interest in the sedentary life and demand to be off. Had it been possible to let our dog wander at will then there would have been no problem. Whilst we were up and walking Boots could usually be off the lead, providing one of us had our running shoes on! If, however, we were trying to have a rest we could not usually relax because his nose invariably led him out of sight and earshot, so that one of us always had to rush off in pursuit.

The occasions when we were able to sit for several hours whilst Boots safely amused himself are clear in my memory, because they were so few and far between. One such time was when the three of us were holidaying in Devon and were spending the day in a village near to Seaton. We had climbed up a hill at the foot of which was a wide stream. On the other side of this stream there was a tea garden overlooking the sea. There was also a large car park, but when we left our car there we were aware that it was simply for the tea gardens and that those who came and went did so slowly and with care, making allowances for playing children and unleashed animals.

The view from the top of the hill was superb, and we really wanted to be able to sit a while in the hot sunshine and relax. But what about Boots? We decided to put him to the test, sat ourselves down and let him off the lead. Immediately he set off down the way we had come, and I was on my feet ready to chase after him. My husband restrained me and suggested we should keep watch to see where our beagle went. He reached the bushes at the bottom of the hill and disappeared. What seemed a very long time afterwards he reappeared on the other side of the stream. We then saw him trot around the car park, vanish again and reappear in the tea gardens. Fortunately it was not tea time and so there were many empty tables. Boots explored underneath these and then paused to ponder awhile. We then saw him, made smaller by the distance, turn around, trot back through the car park, disappear for a few minutes then reappear through the bushes on our side of the stream. Up the hill he then toiled and arrived back with us with tongue hanging out and ready to lie down.

After a brief rest to catch his breath he was up on his feet and popping off again down the hill. As we watched our beagle we saw him repeat, exactly, his previous journey before plodding up the hill once more. The day was very hot, and we were concerned about the effect the heat of the day would have upon Boots. That was only until we became aware that he was taking longer each time to reappear on the other side of the stream. We realized that he must be having a great time paddling and drinking and generally cooling himself down in order to fully enjoy the rest of his adventure.

We sat on that hillside for several hours and were able to relax as Boots repeated his journey down the hill, across the stream, round the car park, through the tea gardens and back again. Each foray took a good twenty minutes and he must have completed at least half a dozen trips before we decided that we would join him and have tea in the gardens. That was a situation that was as safe as we could get in such a perfect setting, and we were never able to find another to match it.

Once or twice we managed to sit awhile and let Boots wander, but that was the only time in over sixteen years when we could really relax knowing that our beagle had found a satisfying adventure that was as safe as it was enjoyable, thus allowing us to feel secure enough to rest and absorb the tranquillity and beauty around us.

8

The rescue

When Boots was nine years old we moved to a bigger house. The back garden of this Victorian town house was completely secure, being enclosed by a high brick wall. We quite quickly made this into an olde worlde garden by planting fast-growing shrubs and climbing roses. We then installed a fountain and bought a suitably lilliputian summer house. In short, we did our utmost to make the garden interesting both for ourselves and for our dog.

Because the houses around us were, like ours, spacious with three reception rooms and four bedrooms, they lent themselves to conversion into flats and this had happened to the house on each side of ours. The flats in one of these houses were owner-occupied, providing us with very kind neighbours whilst the two flats on the other side of us were rented out on short lets. Yet another couple had moved into the ground floor flat, but because they were out all day, we hardly saw them.

Winter came and we began to hear doggie noises from next door's patio (the upstairs flat had the garden). At first we were not concerned because the snuffling and woofling that came over the wall seemed to be quite normal. However, as the winter really set in we started to hear noises that distressed and worried us. By gaining enough height to peer over the wall, I was able to find out that the dog was a crossbreed and that he resembled a large fox. He always seemed to be in trouble and when, one very dark evening, we heard very unhappy doggie noises coming from next door, we climbed up the wall in time to see the man brandishing a large stick at the terrified dog. We remonstrated with him and asked what seemed to be the trouble. He was completely taken by surprise, muttered something, discarded the stick and took the dog inside.

After that we listened even more intently, and I was not surprised to learn from one of the young people lodging in the upstairs flat that they had found the dog left in the very cold, draughty porch with no food, no water and no bedding. The downstairs couple were nowhere to be found and it soon became apparent that this big, fox-like creature was, indeed, terrified of people.

I felt that someone official needed to be involved immediately for the sake of the animal and his future. My suggestion was that the RSPCA should be contacted to ask whether one of their officers could become involved. Because, however, it was a Friday, they enquired whether the dog could be cared for over the weekend and then somebody would come to the flat on the following Monday to assess the whole situation.

There were three young people sharing the upstairs flat – one girl and two young men – all of whom were animal lovers and each of them was very angry because of the way that the downstairs dog had been treated. We decided to share his care over the weekend period, and all, I think, assumed that he would be taken by the RSPCA at the beginning of the next week, with a view to being found a new home.

The dog gradually realized that we meant him no harm and, by late on Saturday afternoon, he agreed to go upstairs to be with the youngsters. I provided meals and helped with the walking.

These walks had to be taken separately from our own dog who had objected vociferously when, quite stupidly, I had walked the dog up our path to collect Boots, planning a happy outing together. No way! Our beagle made it very clear that he would not go out with this intruder that leapt about and behaved so wildly. I should, of course, have introduced them to each other on neutral ground, but having made the mistake, I then spent twice as long out in the wintry air as each dog had his exercise.

All went well until early on the Saturday evening. I had taken the evening meal next door and watched with delight whilst the dog devoured his supper. Returning home to prepare our own meal I was just telling my husband how much less frightened the dog now seemed, when there was a frantic knocking on our front door. The girl from the upstairs flat was on the doorstep. We took her indoors and she breathlessly explained that the downstairs couple had returned and were, at that moment, collecting cases, clothes and various bits of kitchen equipment, obviously about to do a moonlight. Unfortunately the dog was downstairs in the hall as they came in and it had become obvious that they planned to take him with them.

'Please help – we can't just let them take him,' implored the girl from upstairs.

'Of course we can't!' said my husband and I in unison, as we rushed next door without getting outdoor shoes or coats in spite of the wintry weather.

As we erupted onto next door's pathway, the couple were hurrying out to their car and the dog was dervishing around them and generally behaving wildly. My husband, feeling very disadvantaged by his slippers, cardigan and spectacles, demanded to know where the couple were going (really not his business) and what they intended to do about the dog (very much our business). The girl, to whom we assumed the dog belonged, said the creature was going with them in the car. 'To be abandoned again by you?' queried my husband. The girl began to bristle and obviously wanted to be gone as quickly as possible.

She was insistent that she had not deliberately left her dog alone and unattended. He had, she said, run off so they had to go away and leave him, not knowing where he was.

'A likely story,' retorted my husband. 'I suppose he let himself into the porch with the latchkey he had hanging around his neck!'

By this time the luggage had been stowed in their car and the couple were fretting and fussing, obviously wanting to get away.

Whilst this was going on I had managed to stop the dog from being killed on the busy thoroughfare at the end of our residential road, and the man had put him into the car with the cases. My husband, seeing the anguished looks from the girl and myself, was insisting that the female owner of the dog should give him up so that a suitable, caring home could be found for him. She threw the dog's lead at my husband with the words, 'Take him then, I don't want him!' but the man had other ideas. It was equally obvious that he, like his partner, had no warm feelings towards the poor creature imprisoned in their car, but it was also apparent that he was not prepared to be told what to do by this politely dictatorial neighbour. He indicated, not too politely, that the dog was in the car and would stay there. I had other ideas and told him so.

'That dog won't come to you,' he sneered, but, once more, my ideas differed from his. Hoping desperately that the car door would not be locked, I stretched out my hand to his accompanying taunt of – 'He'll have that hand off!' The door opened at my touch.

'Come along darling,' I pleaded, and the over-excited dog leapt out of the vehicle into my outstretched arms. Quickly I handed him over to the young people from the upstairs flat, instructing them to take the dog indoors and into their flat without delay. This they did without question, leaving my husband and I outside with one very annoyed woman and her exceedingly angry man-friend. He swore and then he shouted – at least we assumed the words were uncomplimentary because of his demeanour – we could not understand what he was saying due to his, by now, apoplectic condition. The woman became increasingly anxious to be off but the man, it was obvious, felt that we had got the better of him and he did not like that at all. He continued to shout abuse at us whilst my husband, who was also very angry by this time, tore into him verbally without, I should stress, one single swear word passing his lips. It really was most impressive, especially as the man was considerably larger and taller than my husband.

Whilst this was happening I was, so my husband told me

later, standing in our somewhat select road and shrieking 'like a fishwife'.

Eventually the woman persuaded her friend that there was just no point in continuing the slanging match – she did not want the poor dog anyway – but he was obviously very reluctant to give way to another man! At last even he saw that we were never going to return the dog to them, so he kicked his car whilst seeking a final insult to hurl at us. I had read about people hopping about in a rage and he really had reached that stage. His abuse and his shouting had done nothing to sway the determination of the bespectacled, be-slippered man confronting him. He obviously decided at that point that my husband must be mad and told him so in no uncertain terms, before hurling himself into the car.

They then drove away leaving my husband and I feeling quite exhausted. We looked up and down the dark road fully expecting curtains to be drawn back, lights to be blazing forth and voices to be raised in enquiry. But, no, the road remained in darkness and there was a total stillness which was almost uncanny. We had just lived through one of the most traumatic half hours of our lives and our friends and neighbours were totally unaware of what had happened! We went back indoors to our beagle, put the kettle on and invited the young people from next door to bring the dog round so that we could review the recent events. The dog, not surprisingly, was very overexcited and began to race round our house and garden. What did surprise us was that Boots accepted this wild creature into our home and even decided to join in his mad rushing around.

It was agreed that the dog would stay with us that night because the youngsters had an evening already planned which meant them being away until the early hours of Sunday. We were all rather concerned lest the male half of the 'flitting' couple decided to have another try at getting the dog back. My husband felt this concern so strongly that he telephoned the local Police Station and requested a visit.

Two very helpful constables quickly arrived and heard our story. They repeatedly had to do a quick side-step to avoid being trampled by what appeared to be at least half a dozen dogs! They couldn't believe there were only two animals in our home that night, nor could we persuade the dogs to stand still for long enough to prove our point – that there *were* only two. The policemen promised to take our house into their tour of duty for the night in order to ward off any potential vandalism of house or cars.

Needless to say we did not get much sleep that night. Boots eventually tired of the hectic playtime he was having with the next door dog, and decided to go to bed. When my husband and I tried to settle down we found ourselves continually going over the evening. We had decided to give the dog the run of the house – perhaps unwisely – because we were very aware of his highly-strung and totally over-excited state. He seemed to spend a lot of time in our bedroom, where Boots had his bed. Each time I opened my eyes that night I saw a fox-like face with lolling tongue and pointed ears. He so reminded me of Basil Brush, who was very popular at that time, that I would not have been at all surprised to hear the words 'Boom, boom,' issue from his mouth!

The next morning my husband stayed with the dogs whilst I went off to church. I returned to find the three young people plus several of their friends in the sitting room discussing what type of dog this foxy creature was. When one of them was certain he was an Elk Hound, I really felt they must be looking at him through rose-coloured spectacles.

The plan was, still, to await the arrival of the RSPCA inspector the following day. Meanwhile the dog went back next door via a pub lunch with that very caring group of young people.

9

Adoption

On the following Monday the RSPCA man did, indeed, arrive next door. His visit coincided with a return call made by the offending couple – presumably to collect the rest of their belongings. This really was fortuitous because the inspector interviewed the dog's owner regarding the way in which she had abandoned her pet. She, as was only to be expected, denied having done such a thing. The inspector explained that it would be very difficult to prove ill-treatment but he did obtain the very definite statement from the owner that she no longer wished to keep the dog. The inspector said that, although he would have preferred her comments in writing, he felt able to say that the dog no longer belonged to her and that she would have no claims to him in the future.

By now the three young people next door had become very attached to the said dog and had decided not to let him be taken away to the RSPCA kennels – they would adopt him themselves.

Immediately they gave him a new name. From that day onwards he would be called Benjie. The girl took charge and, with admirable concern, took him to the vet to have his injections. She also queried his age and was told that her new charge was about two years old. It would be untrue to suggest that Benjie began, from that day forward, to live a perfect doggie existence. With hindsight I query what, in a dog's mind, would constitute 'perfection'. I could only compare the life of the dog next door with the way in which Boots arranged his, and our, lives. The two were very different!

Benjie now belonged to a girl and two fellows all in their early twenties. Their hours of work or study were, to say the least, erratic and their leisure time was spent with their friends in pubs and other centres of entertainment.

Visiting the pub became part of Benjie's life and we would hear with trepidation of the ham bones etc. with which he was regularly presented. He was fed well enough, but at very odd hours of the day or night, and he was walked whenever one of the young people felt like some fresh air or remembered that dogs do like to be taken out.

Benjie soon became used to living in the upstairs flat and obviously enjoyed his front window that overlooked our fairly busy road. I did not doubt that the youngsters were very fond of their addition to the household, but I did, nevertheless, become somewhat concerned when the top of that rusty-coloured head seemed to be at the window for hours on end. From the pathway this was all that I could see of him. I would go out in the car and see the top of Benjie's head at the window, and when I returned hours later there it would be, seemingly in the same position. Did he hear my car and rush to the window hoping a member of his family had returned? Did he come to the window to see whether the car was that of his previous owner? Had he really spent all of the time that I was away just standing, or sitting up, and looking out of that same window?

Whenever the young people all planned to be away at the weekend we received a request to 'mind' Benjie. He obviously enjoyed spending time with Boots and it was also obvious that he simply revelled in the long walks that were very much a part of our beagle's life. I shall never forget the first time we took Benjie to a forest in Sussex. Because he was extremely obedient we were able to let him run free, provided we were nowhere near traffic. On this particular outing we were walking with my mother-in-law and a friend along one of the paths through the woods. Boots was exploring and Benjie was some way ahead excitedly running from tree to tree, disappearing into the undergrowth and reappearing further down the path, looking so much like a fox that I was relieved we were not in hunting country!

It was after that particular weekend with us that I really began to question whether the dog next door was having the best life possible. On the Monday which was a Bank Holiday, my husband and I were walking up our road from the seafront. We had Boots and Benjie on their leads and were returning home because the girl from next door was expected back and would be calling to collect her dog.

As we strolled up the road we saw her coming down to meet us. I waited for some reaction from her adopted dog, but there was none. When she reached us she did just acknowledge Benjie, but was more interested in chattering about her own weekend away. We invited her into our garden for coffee and I watched the dog to see how he would behave. It soon became obvious that all he wanted to do was have fun with Boots – he simply ignored his mistress. Eventually she decided to return to her own flat and, not very enthusiastically, took Benjie with her.

I felt decidedly sad and began to wonder whether the girl was regretting her decision to adopt Benjie now that she realised the responsibility, time, expense and general caring that having an animal entails. I am not suggesting that she was not fond of him, but I did wonder whether she regretted her hastily-made decision to keep Benjie.

As it turned out, the dog's stay with the young people next door was not to be a prolonged one. After about five months we learned that they were leaving the upstairs flat and each going their separate ways.

One evening we answered a knock at our door to find Benjie and his mistress needing to talk. In they came and whilst Boots and his doggie visitor proceeded to wreck the sitting room, the girl explained that she had to go into hospital for three weeks to have an operation on her knee. What about Benjie? He was, of course, our immediate concern. We were told that arrangements had been made for him to stay with a friend who lived and worked in a local hotel. We wished them both well, assuming that Benjie would go with his mistress when she went to convalesce at her parents' home. Just over three weeks later we were surprised to receive a visit from the girl, on crutches, and her mother. We soon learned that they had come to explain that Benjie could not go with his mistress – her parents already had a dog and a cat and would not countenance having another animal in their house. The girl did seem genuinely upset at the thought of parting with her dog, and obviously hoped one day to be able to have him back with her. Meanwhile, would it be possible for Benjie to stay with us?

That was on the Friday. My husband and I asked for time to consider this request, because we were not exactly looking for an addition to our family. We then had a traumatic, soul-searching weekend, during which the discussions went as follows – did we really want the expense, responsibility and restraints of having another dog? Would having Benjie in the home really be fair to Boots – after all, he had ruled his, and our, roost for ten years. If we had another dog, would that dog be Benjie? Poor Benjie! Round and round went the words, round and round went our thoughts. If only this decision had not been thrust upon us!

By the end of Sunday we knew what conclusion we had to reach. There really was no choice in this matter – indeed there had never been any element of choice. We had helped to rescue Benjie, had continued to be concerned about him, so how, when he now needed us again, how could we possibly refuse?

We did, however, decide upon one very definite stipulation – Benjie could come and live with us, but it would have to be a permanent arrangement. No ifs, buts, or maybes, because it really was time that this poor animal had a settled home.

My husband telephoned the girl and put this to her. He told her that we would need her to sign an adoption document that would be ready when she brought Benjie to us the following evening. If she felt unable to hand her dog over to us permanently, then perhaps she really did need to sit down and think the matter through more thoroughly. He explained that we could understand that she was reluctant to give Benjie up entirely, but that in view of her own uncertain future, we felt she must try to put her dog's well-being before her own feelings.

Monday evening arrived and four of us sat waiting for our lives to change. My mother-in-law was on one of her regular visits to us at the time, and we were very glad to have her support – she was a caring but also a practical lady – just what was needed at that moment. Earlier in the day my husband had paid a visit to our local branch of Mothercare to purchase a baby gate. We had decided that we needed to be able to separate off various parts of the house, and that, in particular, Benjie must learn to sleep downstairs. We could not have two dogs muscling into the bed each night. He found the assistant most kind and helpful until he let it be known that the gate was to try to control a dog and not for the protection of a baby. She then left my husband to his own devices and went to serve a more conventional customer!

We had the necessary adoption paper ready and Benjie was signed-over to us for the rest of his life. His ex-mistress, as she now was, departed with her mother and we studied our adopted dog.

We were dismayed by his condition. During the preceding three weeks he had only had short walks on the lead and his bedding was so badly soiled that it had to be destroyed. His coat was matted with various things, in particular with chewing gum. He was exceedingly thin. He was also very emotionally wound-up and we were very glad that my mother-in-law would be around all of the time. Benjie kept leaping upon Boots and getting increasingly randy with him. We had learned that this was the one thing our beagle would not accept from another dog, and we realised that over the next few days, being crucial in the forming of a good or bad doggie relationship, the dogs needed to be closely monitored and, indeed, supervised. We were aware of the theory that animals should be left to work out their own relationships, but we did know Boots very well and that knowledge told us that if this unkempt, randy creature kept leaping all over him, our beagle would very soon tell Benjie and us that enough was enough! During the following week my mother-in-law spent hours grooming the new dog. Much of his fur had to be cut away but, when she had finished, we had a much healthier looking creature in our midst. He revelled in his walks, positively gobbled his food, loved Boots and seemed quite fond of us.

We began to find dog chews hidden all over the house. This usually happened at night, and at first we thought that Boots was making sure his new brother didn't make off with any of his prize possessions. This did surprise us because Boots, apart from when he had actually 'stolen' anything, was not a possessive dog. We later learned that it was Benjie who was taking and hiding the chews, and we realised that he had not been used to such delights in his sad and troubled life. As he gradually built up his very own store of goodies, he became less acquisitive and was able to let Boots' chews stay in the toy basket. Benjie was quite bright in some ways but somewhat dull in others. One example of this was the incident of the two life-size greyhounds, carved from wood, that suddenly began to leak! Boots had chosen from the very beginning to treat these dogs with the contempt that anything without the correct smell attached deserved. From the day when I had arrived home from the auction with one under each arm Boots had completely ignored them. After Benjie's arrival, however, I repeatedly found a large puddle around the base of each dog in turn. As fast as I cleared up the wet, another puddle appeared. We eventually realized that our new live dog was very definitely marking the two 'dead' ones and telling them in no uncertain terms that this was his territory and not theirs! Until he became more settled and felt more secure with us we put the dogs on top of cupboards at least eight feet high – even Benjie's determination and enthusiasm could not reach that far!

10

A new lease of life

By the time that we adopted Benjie our beagle had passed his tenth birthday. Now that he had reached double figures, and working on the generally accepted theory that seven human years equal one doggie year, Boots could, surely, be considered as elderly. Had he still been our only dog we should probably have been looking for signs of slowing down, although as he was a beagle such signs might not have been very obvious.

No so, however, because even if Boots had been thinking about slipping gently into a quieter lifestyle, the eruption into our lives of this fox-like crossbreed called Benjie meant that Boots became very young again. I don't mean to give the impression that he went back to his puppy ways – indeed his generosity with his toys and his general forbearance were magnificently mature! Benjie was allowed to take Boots' toys, chew his chews and generally make a nuisance of himself. When he became too boisterous and overbearing, Boots showed his teeth to great effect, and Benjie then knew that enough was enough and he must back off.

All seemed to be well during those first few months, and, as our vet had told us, the two dogs appeared to be working out their relationship without too much trouble.

Benjie had been with us for several months before there were any signs of trouble and strife. Each Sunday evening, after church, we would have our bread and butter tea – the highlight of my husband's week – and Boots would have a Bonio. Of course, Benjie soon became used to this treat and as soon as the tea things appeared he would sit, ears pricked and tongue lolling, waiting for the Bonios to appear. One Sunday the biscuits had been handed out, and my husband and I were about to draw our chairs up to the table, when, suddenly, teeth were bared, fur was flying and our two dogs were rolling around the breakfast room floor locked in very serious combat!

We were so amazed that, for the moment, we froze. Then I screamed, being the emotional one, and my husband, the calmly practical one, did something about it. He quickly realized that this was a real dog fight. Not wanting to have his hand bitten, he grabbed his chair, forced it between the two animals and, quite literally, managed to prise them apart. Boots was extremely upset, and his back fur was standing up as he walked away from the scene with very stiff legs. Benjie, on the other hand, was excited but not particularly fussed. I, also, was extremely excited and very, very fussed, as I decided that the two dogs would never again be able to be left together unsupervised and that this lovely brotherly relationship seemed to have completely disintegrated!

We worked out that the problem had arisen because one of the dogs had had designs on the other one's Bonio, but we never did know which of them muscled in. What was, however, very apparent, was that the other dog retaliated immediately and very aggressively.

Boots took some time to recover from the set-to, which made us think that it was probably the beagle that tried to grab two Bonios for himself, and that Benjie, normally so quick to back off, was definitely not prepared to part with his food or goodies.

By the end of the evening things seemed to have returned to normal, but for several Sundays afterwards Boots became stiff-legged and defensive when the Bonios appeared and we made certain to be around until every crumb had been eaten.

The only other time that the two of them had a real fight was also over food. They had their main meal of the day in separate parts of the kitchen. Benjie always ate more slowly than Boots, who would creep around the corner and stand behind Benjie waiting for some bits to fall from his plate. We always made

A new lease of life

certain that Boots kept his distance, though, because it seemed so unfair to Benjie to have his brother breathing down his neck whilst he was eating. About two months after the incident of the Bonios however, Boots could not contain himself and he got just that bit too close to our adopted dog's supper. Once again the fur flew! Fortunately, my father, who was staying with us, was nearby. He is very used to dogs and their ways, and never panics. He quickly separated the two dogs and order was once more restored. Although Boots had learned that the one thing designed to make Benjie very cross was to try to take his food, and although our new dog had asserted his authority in this respect, in every other way our beagle continued to be top dog.

Benjie really loved his walks and Boots obviously enjoyed introducing his new brother to his own familiar and special places. Whereas we always needed to know where our beagle was, which was usually a considerable distance in front of us, our new dog liked to know where we were. He was always very interested in all that Boots had to show him, but when he sensed that we were being left too far behind he would very quickly come back and shadow our footsteps.

When we adopted Benjie we were aware that his former mistress might well want to see him sometimes. The one stipulation that we made was that she should not call at the house without prior warning. This was because we did not know at that stage how Benjie would react to seeing her and we certainly did not want her peering through the window at him. That would, we know, have caused great concern to Boots which would have excited his new brother – with what resulting chaos we could only hazard a guess.

Three weeks after Benjie's arrival and, fortunately, on a day when I was not at work, his previous mistress arrived on the doorstep without, of course, any warning. The two dogs rushed to the door and by the time I became aware of the situation, they were both going mad. I tried to make her feel welcome, but had to remonstrate with her for not attempting to abide by our request about letting us know of her intended visit. Benjie's behaviour was very strange. He sat close to me the whole hour or so that his previous owner was with us and, during that time, he barked solidly. Not his usual lovely woof-woof, but a high-pitched somewhat hysterical bark, and there was simply no way in which I could stop him. Was he wild with delight at seeing her again and, if so, why did he not jump around or, at least, sit close to her? On the other hand, was he behaving so frantically because he thought she had come to take him away from his new life he so obviously enjoyed? We shall never know. Suffice it to say that we heard nothing further from her. Whether that was because she was not prepared to make an appointment to see Benjie, whether it was because I had not succeeded in making her feel welcome, whether she realized that, as far as we were concerned, the adoption was final or whether she simply forgot him, we shall never know. I do know, however, that we were relieved when nothing further was heard from her, because we felt so strongly that Benjie needed space to make a new life and to forge new bonds.

Although Boots appeared able to take or leave this addition to the family, the arrival of Benjie gradually turned our beagle into a young dog again. Any signs of staidness disappeared as the challenge of having another dog in the home began to have its effect.

Benjie continued to thrive. We had wanted to change his name to go with his new life but felt that would be unfair. After all, he had gone through a name-change only six months previously. Gradually, however, the Benjie became Bennie, Ben or Benjamin, the latter being used when he needed a gentle reprimand. Somehow it seemed possible to make 'Benjamin' sound as though a modicum of discipline was being included in the name, whereas 'Bennie' or 'Ben' always seemed totally untrammelled.

Our regular visits to the New Forest continued and it was a real delight to see Bennie's interest and excitement increase as the thrills of the forest were introduced to him.

As on our walks near to our home, Bennie was only prepared to follow Boots a certain distance into a new place or adventure. He would then remember my husband and I and would hasten back to walk with us for a while. We soon learned that our new dog loved water and the ever-present streams in the forest afforded him much pleasure. He was also absolutely fascinated by culverts of which there are many in the forest. Often the path will be crossed by an underground pipe. These come in assorted sizes – small, medium or large and dog-sized. Sometimes they are dry, sometimes they are muddy and on some joyful occasions they have a stream flowing through. It was the latter that thrilled Bennie the most. The dry culverts he could take or leave, indeed he still can, but those with water had to be thoroughly explored. Although in many ways Bennie was very timid, he would disappear without hesitation into these underground streams and on many occasions we have felt

... two excited, agitated tails, but no heads to be seen

a moment's panic as we have turned to the spot where our cross-bred was last seen, only to find ourselves staring with disbelief at a deserted pathway.

Although, as I have said, Boots continued very much to do his own thing on our walks, especially in the New Forest, it soon became apparent that the presence of another dog in our family really revitalised our beagle.

Bennie quickly became very attached to Boots and liked to be where he was – providing, of course, that we were not too far away. In the home situation it did not matter where we were, as long as our adopted dog knew that his brother was around.

Boots began to turn out his toy basket with extra zest when Bennie was around to take an interest. Regularly we would go into the sitting room and find two excited, agitated tails but no heads to be seen. These were both buried deep inside the toy basket which was in fact, a very large log basket. Bennie had to be taught how to play with these various and varied toys, and many were the games we all had as we shared in his enjoyment. The best place indoors for these games was the sitting room. This was a very long room, being two large rooms made into one. The amazing thing was that, although rugs and cushions went flying, only one antique cup and saucer came to grief. It was my fault entirely, because I had hurled a ball too vigorously and too high. Boots jumped to get said ball which bounced onto a side table and shot the tiny porcelain cup high into the air; I fielded it then lost my grip and dropped it onto the floor. It shattered into four separate pieces. My husband stuck it together but its value had, of course disappeared.

Incidents like that really frightened Bennie, who always seemed to expect to be punished. Boots, of course, did not know the meaning of that kind of fear, and we were always hugging our new dog to reassure and comfort him. That meant that Boots had double his normal number of caresses, but, as previously, he would sometimes accept these signs of affection from us but, more often, he would shrug them off and continue with what he was doing.

11

Too tired to go on

We had various traumas through Boots' early teen years, that usually meant a visit to the vet so that our beagle could be restored to his normal healthy self. My husband used to point out to me, and to the vet, that Boots was the reason why we had an old banger and the vet had the latest Merc. – or whatever was in vogue at the time! We didn't begrudge the amount of money spent on vet's fees because we only wanted the very best treatment for our dogs.

At the age of eleven Boots developed a heart murmur. At first we were very over-conscious of this and wanted to wrap him up in cotton wool. However, we did eventually take our vet's advice and let Boots continue to go his own way, and do his own thing. What other way was there for a beagle to go? He had his medication each day and continued to rush around like a two year old. What we did begin to notice, however, was that Boots did not recover quite so quickly from a skirmish with another dog, or from evacuating, one way or the other, from his doggie system any foreign body he had eaten. Being a beagle he continued to chew things all of his life and slippers and tights were amongst his favourite 'treats'. My husband seemed to spend most of Boots' years with us walking around with sorely damaged slippers. I was always having to replenish my tights, drawer, because no matter how often I planned to keep these away from our beagle, he regularly out-witted me. It was this wayward behaviour that nearly cost Boots his life and nearly ruined a very special day in our family.

I had been studying for some years with the Open University and the day dawned when, I could hardly believe it, I was to graduate with a B.A. degree. That was the Saturday and the following day was our wedding anniversary and a very dear friend's ninety-fifth birthday. Altogether it would be a memorable weekend!

On the previous Friday I had been careless with a pair of bright red tights and Boots had wrought havoc with them. I was cross about the loss of those particular tights, but not worried about our beagle because I did not think he had actually swallowed much of the nylon material.

On the Saturday morning we were up very early because my husband had to make a round trip of one hundred and twenty miles to collect my family for the very special occasion. It became apparent during breakfast that all was not well with our beagle. He tried repeatedly to be sick, obviously needing to evacuate something from his system. Try as he would he could get no further than blowing himself up like a balloon – something he did when wanting to vomit.

I then walked him along the road, hoping that the exercise would produce some results. Success; as we returned to the house he brought up some violent red matter which my husband, being unaware of the colour of the previous day's tights, thought was blood. I was able to hastily reassure him about that, but we then realised that Boots was on the point of collapse and rushed him round to the vet. We were taken immediately into the consulting room where we were told that our lad, due partly to straining and partly to his advanced years, was severely dehydrated and a very sick dog.

We were devastated and when the vet said that Boots must stay at the surgery and immediately be put onto a drip I tearfully pointed out that our beagle must die at home. The vet did not give us false assurances that Boots was not going to die, but he did say that he would be 'on call' all of the weekend and would keep a very close watch on our beagle. Boots was then very quickly wrapped in a blanket and conveyed to the treatment part of the premises.

By this time I had decided that Graduation Day was definitely a non-starter and that only Boots and his welfare mattered. Not so! Once the vet and his equally caring receptionist had realized the importance of the day, they were both determined that the 'show must go on'. Spurred on by their encouragement we hurried back home and my husband set out to collect the family nearly two hours later than planned. I telephoned home, my father answered, I burst into tears and he said 'I'll get your mother'. The talk with my mother had a most calming effect upon me and the day began to come together again.

The telephone lines between our house and the veterinary practice were red hot that day, but just before the graduation ceremony began, my husband gave me the 'thumbs-up' sign across the auditorium conveying the news that Boots was responding to treatment and holding his own.

When we went to collect him after church the following day, Boots came to greet us, a little wobbly on his legs but ready once more to face the world. He very soon went from the light diet prescribed, to his normal beagle-type food, and his strength and energy quickly returned to normal.

What, we did learn however, was that Boots at fifteen years of age was more vulnerable and less resistant to self-inflicted beagle injury.

About a year after the episode of the red tights we were visiting a friend and went walking in her local woods. Bennie and Boots were hithering and thithering in their usual fashion, and we three humans were strolling along chatting about family events and local gossip. An elderly gentleman came towards us with his Labrador – a beige coloured, rather overweight creature. The owner of this dog courteously passed the time of day with us and walked on, and the dog also passed by. Whether our beagle threw out an insult as the Labrador walked by, we shall never know. Suffice it to say that suddenly Boots was upside down in a ditch with the hefty dog on top of him. We once more realized that Boots was becoming less solid and less able to defend himself. Fortunately my husband dived into the writhing mass and hauled the attacking dog away –

before Bennie had time to size up the situation and throw his enthusiasm into the fray.

At first we continued with our walk, thinking that Boots would calm down more quickly if we behaved normally. We then discovered, however, that our beagle had been bitten in at least four places. Two hours later he went into a state of deep shock.

Once more he was rushed to the vet who decided to treat the shock and try to forestall the onset of pneumonia. The bites, he felt, could take care of themselves. Again Boots recovered, but we were very wary from then on when big dogs came near to him. We felt that a further mugging might really damage him.

The incident I have just related took place in the autumn of Boots' seventeenth year, and in December of that same year we began, once more, to feel concern about our dog's well-being. Unlike any beagle, Boots became very fussy about his food, and we had to really tempt him to eat enough to keep his beagle frame in action.

The doggie menu at our house was far more interesting and varied than the human one! Each day Boots was invited to choose between steak, lamb casserole, special fried rice, various fish dishes – to name but a few. He usually agreed to accept one of the items offered, but his choice was never the same two days in succession. In spite of our efforts to feed him, we could see that Boots was becoming increasingly frail. But he was a beagle, and beagles do not easily give up the fight! When he decided that the only solid food he wanted was Maltesers, we popped these into his mouth unceasingly. These did not, of course, do much to sustain him, and he willingly accepted chicken Complan and Brands Essence. On the 26th of January, a lovely sunny day, Boots had a dig in the garden, investigated the pond, sniffed all of the smells and seemed to have really overcome the chest infection that had been causing extra concern. 'We'll have him for a while yet,' we said to each other.

It was not to be.

On the 27th of January, 1989, Boots died.

We realized early that morning that something had

changed. Our beagle refused all sustenance and was barely able to stand without help.

We tucked him back into his bed, looked at each other and accepted, with sinking hearts, that he was telling us that he was just too tired to go on.

Boots had not really had an old-age, because he was always much too busy and too interested in life. In spite of his advanced years, he had not seemed old. Now, however, we knew what we had to do. We had to put into practise our firm belief that one of the greatest acts of love is being able to let go, and knowing when to do this. So it was that one of our kindly, compassionate vets came to our home and gently helped our beagle to go to sleep.

We were devastated! For nigh-on seventeen years Boots had allowed us to share his life, with its excitements and its traumas. They were not peaceful years – how could they be as he was a beagle! They were, however, lively and full years. God had allowed us to have Boots for longer than could be expected, and so we tried not to complain about the hurt and emptiness that overwhelmed us. But, as my husband was to say repeatedly during the following days, 'How we will be able to organize our lives without our beagle being in charge, we do not know.'

The next day we drove up country with Boots, tucked into his bed, on the back seat. It was so hard to believe that he would not suddenly wake up and demand to know where we were.

We arrived at the place where his little body was to be cremated and were greeted with warmth and kindly consideration. We planted a last kiss on that still-silky beagle brow and left him lying in a summerhouse set on a quiet lawn surrounded by hedges and trees. Although we felt strongly that it was only his body that we were leaving, it was comforting to be so sure that his earthly remains would continue to be treated with dignity and gentleness after our departure. My husband was to make a return visit a few days later to collect Boots' ashes. In mid-February these were to travel with us to his much-loved New Forest. Over that weekend and during the following weeks we were comforted and supported by numerous telephone calls from family and friends. Each post brought letters and cards. There was the bunch of flowers on my desk, the telephone removed from my hand when the conversation became too difficult, and the thoughts deliberately not spoken aloud because, in those first days, we felt so vulnerable.

We were both surprised and deeply touched by so much caring and realized that our stubborn, wilful, adventurous beagle had touched many lives other than our own.

12

Free to roam in the forest he loved

We had never before, as a couple, had to decide what to do with the ashes of a much-loved pet. Perhaps instinctively we felt that the remains of our Boots should be scattered in a place where he had always enjoyed himself. As our beagle had a vast capacity for getting joy from whatever outing presented itself, there were numerous places on offer. However, the area that so regularly drew us was, of course, the New Forest.

Before making a final and irrevocable decision we had to discuss various other possibilities. Should we bury the casket in our garden? Definitely not, because Bennie would, almost certainly, choose the place of interment to dig one of his huge holes and that would be distressing indeed!

Although I was only too aware that the ashes we had collected from the crematorium were only our dog's earthly remains, I still, in those first days, felt the need of something tangible – something that was still Boots.

Realizing our dilemma, my mother suggested that the ashes should be buried in my parents' very large garden where their cats would not unearth them and where there would be just one more doggie grave.

We considered this suggestion and really did appreciate the offer, but my husband was certain that Boots' ashes should be scattered in one of our favourite Forest places. I acquiesced and hoped that when the time came I would be able to part with our little lad's remains. My husband, a very understanding man, assured me that if, at the last moment I changed my mind, then we would bring the ashes back home and think again. So it came about that on a dull February morning we packed the car, having booked a room at a small hotel familiar to ourselves and our dogs.

Before our departure the telephone rang repeatedly. 'Bon Voyage,' from one dog-loving friend conveyed a wealth of meaning. 'Find peace in the Forest,' said another. But perhaps the most touching was from my mother urging us to be very sure of our feelings before scattering the ashes as she reminded us of my family's offer of a grave in their garden for Boots' resting place.

We were a sad little party, over-conscious as we were of the gap in our midst. For ever, or so it seemed that day, we had been four, but now we were only three. At first we followed the usual travelling procedure that had evolved through the years of journeying with our beagle.

We stopped at well-trodden woods for coffee but, as Boots was not there to insist, we did not draw into the motorway services area for tea. This seemed only to magnify our loss as we remembered the great delight our beagle had always taken in car parks and lay-bys.

We had planned to stay in the Forest for several days, giving time to visit favourite spots and time to walk down many memory lanes.

The second day of our stay seemed to be set fair. It was one of those cool, clear days that sometimes come in winter – bright and sunny. It was a clean, fresh, sparkling kind of day. We got into the car, with Bennie, and drove to a well-known car park and from there we set out on foot to my husband's favourite place in the Forest. I love it too – it's impossible not to do so. On one side of the grassy path the trees are thick and impenetrable, whilst on the opposite side there is a variety of trees and shrubs with wide open spaces covered in cushion-like mosses. A place of tranquillity and beauty.

We walked up hill and down dale, scattering Boots' ashes to right and to left. There was nobody there to see the seeds, checked very thoroughly and ascertained to be harmless to animals, that we sowed along the way.

I prayed so hard that they would grow, wanting quite desperately to see clusters of flowers blooming there in the summer that was to come. We had often wondered why a particular shrub or a different type of tree had grown up in a certain spot, but now we wondered whether others, too, had wanted to mark a very special place.

We watched and were sure we saw his beagle tail zig-zagging along the way ahead. We pictured him, nose down, tail up intent only upon the scent of the moment. We looked until our aching eyes could look no longer and then we stood still in that beautiful place and, yet again, said 'Thank you' to God for that so special gift He had given to us.

We wept a great deal that day.

Eventually we returned to the place where we had parked the car. I turned round and saw my husband walking towards the surrounding trees. 'I saved just a few for here,' he said. How fitting that was, because however much our beagle enjoyed his walks, he was always first back in the car park, hoping to find some forbidden treasure before we could catch up with him. What had always been known as my husband's favourite walk became, that day, 'Boots' Special Place'.

13

Afterwards

Ben, from the time we first met him, had always had Boots. We felt increasingly through the years that the reason Bennie settled and adjusted so well was because Boots was around. He was always there to guide, sometimes spoil, reprimand and generally oversee our adopted dog. It was, therefore, quite natural for our concern about how Bennie would cope to be very interwoven with our grief at the departure of our beloved beagle.

On the day that Boots died, our Bennie was very much in evidence, seemingly unaware that the family was being emotionally torn apart. The following day, as I have already described, we left Bennie at home whilst we took Boots' body to be cremated. We made a very definite point of letting Ben peer into the bed as we were leaving the house. We had expected some reaction, but a quick look and an even quicker sniff were all that seemed to be necessary before Bennie turned away and walked into the sitting room. It was as though he was telling us that what we were taking away with us in the car meant nothing to him. He had known and lived with an active, vibrant, get-into-mischief hound, and the little body in the dog bed had nothing to do with Bennie's energetic companion of the past six and a half years.

During the next few months we did our utmost to make certain that Bennie should not pine for his beagle companion. My husband was, at that time, going through an employment

... our Ben ... paying due attention to the sermon!

crisis. Difficult though this was for us all it did mean that he spent a lot of time at home. Everywhere that his master went, Bennie went too. Our fox-like dog was to be seen all over the town where we lived, either walking with his master or tied to a suitable post or pole waiting for said master to reappear from shop or office.

Bennie loved the attention and whereas he had inclined towards being a mother's boy, he now became most definitely his master's shadow. He simply was not given the time nor the opportunity to feel lonely. Perhaps that was a mistake – who can say? Certainly it seemed right to us at the time.

In those days the only time that Ben was left at home alone was when we went to church, although I did warn our minister that one day he might look down from the pulpit and see our Ben, ears pricked, tongue lolling, paying due attention to the sermon!

This regime seemed to pay off. Bennie appeared to be contented and well-adjusted. Whilst being glad that we did not have a wasting dog desperately missing Boots, to cope with, I did find it extremely hard to accept that Bennie could so easily, or so it seemed, get over the loss of his 'brother'.

We continued to visit Boots' special walk every time we went to the New Forest. It was a bitter sweet experience each time we walked that way, but we could not fail to notice that Bennie particularly enjoyed himself on those occasions. He did not, as was his wont, stay close to us. Instead he would run hither and thither amongst the trees, forage excitely in the undergrowth and, when we stopped at one very special place, he would roll around in the fallen leaves. Bennie's bright eyes and generally happy demeanour during those walks was not only interesting, it was also comforting to us both.

My mother firmly believed that Bennie met-up with his 'brother' in that part of the Forest and who is to say she was not right? Certainly my husband and I would not have been at all surprised to see that beagle tail flicking it's way through the bushes!

As the year following Boots' death wore away we continued to watch for signs of some kind of lack in our other dog. But no, he continued to thrive. That was during the first year after Boots died, and we really did think that Bennie had simply walked through that experience without a backward glance.

However, as we entered the second year without our beagle, Ben began to exhibit some unusual traits. He had always been interested in other dogs, and was ever willing to join in a game, especially a race and tear one. He was even more willing to leap into any doggie brawl that he encountered, and even on occasion was the instigator of a fracas. We had, at times, been decidedly embarrassed when our beagle and our fluffy one ganged up against another poor unsuspecting creature!

To see our Bennie running away from dogs wanting to play, and to have him positively clinging to my husband and I for protection was rather upsetting. We wondered whether this was delayed reaction to losing his 'brother' and began to ask ourselves whether it was right to have a solitary dog. Many discussions and much heart-searching later we came to the decision that Bennie was suffering from lack of doggie companionship at home and needed one of his own that he could relate to. It seemed that our human company was not enough.

14

And then came Joe

Having decided that Bennie needed a companion we then had to tackle the next hurdle and agree upon where we should go to find him.

We were in full agreement about the 'him', feeling that as Bennie had been so happy with Boots, we should stick with the male of the species. Nor did we argue about the possible age of said dog, again feeling that Bennie would like a 'brother' of similar age to himself. Where we could not agree was on the type of dog that we should be seeking. At first I went along with the idea that any size, shape, colour or condition of dog would do, and with this in mind my husband visited our local branch of the RSPCA.

He was brought up short by their ruling that as we already had a dog, they would only let us have a bitch. As it was a dog that we wanted, my husband then contacted The National Canine Defence League. They would need to visit our home and assess whether we would be suitable, or acceptable, as adoptive parents to one of their dogs, but that seemed to be the only rule. No problem there because we assumed, I hope correctly, that we would definitely be considered adoption-worthy. However, the delay caused by the RSPCA turn-down had given me time to rethink the situation.

My thoughts went as follows: Boots was irreplaceable but Boots was a beagle. Bennie needed another companion and Bennie had been very happy with his beagle 'brother'. There must be beagles needing a home – perhaps an abundance of beagles looking for adoption – why, therefore, were we not seeking out one of this band of lost and unwanted beagles as Bennie's new companion?

I hurled these thoughts at my husband, who positively blanched. He had loved our beagle dearly but could remember all too clearly the tussles of wills that had been part of each and every day. 'No, no, not another beagle,' he said. I pleaded, I cajoled and, to my shame, I blackmailed. I then obtained the Kennel Club directory of dog rescue organizations. Listed there, as I already knew it would be, was 'Beagle Welfare'. My husband, a very wise man, knew the fight was lost! Having submitted to the inevitable, he put all effort possible into tracking down a dog beagle aged ten, or thereabouts.

Beagle Welfare told us of several beagles in need of a home. There were the two brothers, aged two years, who needed to be homed together. I almost succumbed, but my husband, having agreed to another beagle, really did draw the line at two of that breed, especially such youthful ones! Then there was a six year old dog, also in Hampshire, and I was half way out of the door to get in the car, but was, once more, detained by my husband. Having set his mind to the matter he was determined to stick with the search for a beagle of similar age to Bennie.

The welfare lady with whom we were liaising at that point was equally determined, being certain that she would find what we were looking for. She told us that older male beagles were particularly hard to place.

Succeed she did! A week or so after our first telephone call she contacted us to say that there was a ten year old male beagle in kennels in County Durham. He was in need of a home, preferably where there was another dog. We, however, lived in Sussex. That was no problem, we were told, because the Beagle Welfare network was about to spring into action. The plan was as follows: The Sheerness welfare lady, with whom we had been liaising, would be travelling the following weekend to a dog show in Nottingham: the County Durham welfare lady, who owned the kennels where the beagle was housed, would also be going to the dog show. Simple really –

And then came Joe

the beagle would travel to Nottingham then be handed over to journey to Sheerness. He would spend the Saturday night there and on the Sunday my husband would travel to Sheerness in Kent to collect the dog and bring him back to our home in Sussex. We had to wait a whole week for this handover to take place and during that time the telephone lines between Sussex, Sheerness and County Durham were red hot!

We learned that Joe, for that was his unpretentious name, had been bred at the County Durham kennels. At the age of seven months he was bought by a couple living in Coventry who knew the owner of these kennels very well and whose previous beagle had died at the great age of seventeen and a half years. Joe had obviously gone to a wonderful home where he would have lived out the whole of his life in sheer contentment. Sadly, however, his master died in the January as Joe was to become ten years old in the May. His mistress tried to cope with her healthy, energetic dog, but due to her own poor health she simply could not give him the exercise and attention that he needed. She then made a very brave and unselfish decision. Knowing that, if Joe was to have the lifestyle he deserved and to which he had been accustomed, she had to find him another home, she handed him over to Beagle Welfare and he went back to the kennels where he was born. He had been there for about six weeks when we made our telephone call to begin the search for another beagle.

My heart ached when I heard this sad story. It ached for Joe's mistress who, so soon after saying her earthly farewells to her husband, should then have to part with their much-loved dog. But I must confess that my heart ached even more for that poor creature. Having lost his master he then had to part with his mistress and his lovely home. His world must have collapsed around his beagle ears, and I couldn't wait to draw him into the warmth and security of our home, as I wondered what emotional adjustments we would have to help him to make.

At last the day arrived when the handover was to take place. Immediately after morning church I thrust a lunch box into my husband's hands and Bennie and I sent him off to Sheerness to collect Joe. At six o'clock that evening I took Bennie to our local recreation ground – always one of his favourite haunts – and there we awaited the arrival. We had decided that it would be best if the two dogs met on neutral ground so that we could then all arrive home together.

Bennie and I were circumnavigating the rec. for the fourth time and our lovely fluffy dog was becoming somewhat bewildered. It was long past supper time and his mum showed no signs of getting into the car and going back home.

At last – across the green, beyond the trees, I saw my husband come through the hedge. But where was the dog? I then realized that straining away at the end of a fully extended lead was a hound. Bennie and I rushed towards the new arrivals to be greeted by my husband and totally ignored by a lean-looking beagle.

He was, to my intense relief, not at all like Boots. He was taller and longer and altogether less compact. He continued to ignore his new family until we all sat on a bench and I produced some chocolate. We then discovered that we had adopted an extremely vocal beagle! In the ensuing weeks the whole of our locality was to hear our addition to the family. Bennie and Joe simply accepted each other without making any fuss about it. Just as when Bennie was the new dog and Boots had definitely shown that he was there first and would continue to be top dog, it was interesting to witness Bennie exerting his authority and pointing out in no uncertain terms that Joe would be accepted into the family but had to know his place. The few fights that we had to break up were, as with Boots and Bennie in the past, caused by one dog trying to take the other one's food. We were more used to this the second time around, and I did not suffer the same anguish about relationships being damaged and feelings being permanently hurt!

I was really relieved when, on being introduced to Joe, one of our vets said 'He isn't a bit like Boots, is he?' I examined these feelings of relief and realized that they came from a sheer determination not to let any creature detract in any way from the very special place that Boots had always occupied in our lives. Nevertheless, it was not long before Joey had made his own impact – and I do mean impact – not only upon our family but also upon our friends and acquaintances. No beagle can be ignored, but Joey seemed to make a point of imposing his presence upon all within earshot. We learned that there was a strong hunting strain somewhere in his ancestry and this soon became apparent. Whenever he picked up the scent he would lift up that lovely beagle head and bay his feelings to the neighbourhood. He also shouted, loudly, for anything that he wanted, especially for food!

Sometimes Bennie would look at my husband and I with such an appalled expression on his face that we felt sure he was asking us what on earth we thought we had done by bringing this vociferous creature into the home.

Generally speaking, though, the two dogs seemed happy with each others company and, surprisingly, the family once more felt complete. I say 'surprisingly' because I had continued to believe that our family circle would remain permanently broken after Boots died. Joey in no way replaced our first beagle, but his presence certainly helped to ease the hurt and to enable us to once more enjoy the happy times we had experienced with Boots.

EPILOGUE

He'll always be with us

We still visit the New Forest whenever the opportunity arises. It will always be our favourite area, because it is there that we find peace and refreshment – two increasingly important commodities in our busy and somewhat stressful lives.

Like Boots in the past, Bennie and Joe are always excited and happy to see the first trees of the Forest and, also like Boots, they know so many of our walks and picnic places, and greet them joyously. Needless to say, we return often to Boots' special place. It is beautiful at all seasons of the year. Even if we only have time to stay for one night in the Forest, we make sure that we walk his particular walk.

The seeds that I planted there did not grow. They were obviously alien to that part of the woods. This became such an ongoing disappointment to us that my husband said very firmly one day that we had to re-think the situation. We found ourselves spending the whole of the walk desperately studying the various and varied plant life hoping against hope that some of the leaves would look like the picture on the seed packet. They never did, and downcast faces and heavy hearts were the result. In short, all pleasure had gone out of our visits to that particular part of the Forest. It was when he realized what had happened that my husband put his foot down and stated that we must review how and what we felt about a memorial to our beagle.

We now walk more contentedly along this meandering

woodland path because we know that we shall come to a beech tree, standing well back from the track, bearing the inscription 'BOOTS – 1972–1989'. When it was just ourselves and Bennie, we could spend time in this place. Bennie would root amongst the leaves and the fir trees, whilst my husband and I would walk down our memory lane – with laughter and with tears. Life has changed somewhat since Joey came because he too is a beagle and, therefore, always impatient to get on. The tree means nothing to him, and so our visits are now, of necessity, brief, and as we rejoin the path through the Forest we realize afresh that the gap left by our first beagle can never be filled. I agree with those dog lovers who say that, no matter how much one cares about each and every one of the creatures that share one's life, there is always an extra special dog that, somehow, stands out from the others, and the time we shared with our first beagle has left its mark in various and varied ways.

For so many years we walked with Boots through a wealth of experiences. There were the happy and the sad, the pleasant and the painful, the anxious and the reassuring. We shared them all with him and it has been so hard to live with the void he left behind.

Bennie and Joey are, of course, wonderful! Each has made his own place in our lives and in the family. They are both very special, but I'm certain that if, in the years to come I am asked the question 'Was there a particularly special dog in your life?' the name 'BOOTS' would be passed my lips before I had even had time to consider the question.

That is just the way it is.